Indian Nations

THE POMO

by
Edward D. Castillo

General Editors
Herman J. Viola and David Jeffery

A Rivilo Book

RAINTREE
STECK-VAUGHN
PUBLISHERS

A Harcourt Company

Austin · New York
www.steck-vaughn.com

Dedicated to my children, Suelumatra, Cassandra, and Andrew Castillo

Published by Raintree Steck-Vaughn Publishers, an imprint of the Steck-Vaughn Company

Developed for Steck-Vaughn Company by Rivilo Books

Editors: David Stern	Raintree Steck-Vaughn Publishers Staff
Photo Research: Paula Dailey	Publishing Director: Walter Kossmann
Design: Barbara Lisenby and Todd Hirshman	Editor: Kathy DeVico
Electronic Preparation: Lyda Guz	Electronic Production: Scott Melcer

Photo Credits: Gray Barker: cover, 35 bottom; Lisa Ranallo Horse Capture: illustration: pp. 4, 6, 7; © Ilka Hartmann: pp. 8 (artifact courtesy of the Anthropological Studies Center, Sonoma State University), 12 left, 16, 21, 24 right, 26, 28, 30 all, 31, 32 all, 34, 35 top, 36, 39, 40, 41 all, 42 all, 46; Choris (lithograph), pp. 10, 11; William Smith: p. 12 right; Northwind Picture Archives: p. 14; Edward S. Curtis/National Geographic Image Collection: pp. 18, 24 left; Courtesy of Bancroft Library Photo Archives, University of California, Berkeley: Theodora Kroeber, Albert Elsasser, Robert F. Heizer (editors), Ballena Press, 1977, "Drawn From Life, California Indians in Pen and Brush"/illustration number 255, p. 19; illustration number 158: p. 25; R.E. Wood, Courtesy of Bancroft Library, University of California, Berkeley: p. 20 bottom; Photo by Carleton Watkins, 1860, California State Library, Sacramento, California: p. 20 top; Lowie Museum of Anthropology, University of California, Round Valley Indian School, Mendocino, California: p. 22 all; Photo by O. E. Meddaugh, 1902, Courtesy of Historical Society of Lake County, Lakeport, California: p. 27; Whitney Jocelyn-Annin SC: p. 29; Courtesy of the Grace Hudson Museum, city of Ukiah, California: *The Coyote's Coming*, 1898 oil on canvas 24 x 18, Grace Hudson Museum, gift of the Ivan B. and Elvira Hart Trust: p. 33; © Peeter Vilms: p. 37.

Acknowledgments: Thanks to Lanny Pinola; Mabel McKay; Essie Parrish; Tom Renick; Agnes James Fiester; YOKAYO Traditional Pomo Dancers and Singers; Intertribal Pomo Dancers and Singers; Dr. Adrian Praetzellis, Jim Quinn, Gina George (Anthropological Studies Center, Archaeological Collections Facility, Sonoma State University, Rohnert Park, California); Naomi Lynn Fox, Director /Jessie Peter Museum, Santa Rosa Junior College, Santa Rosa, California; Leslie Clair Mankiller-Mendoza (Penobscot); Dennis Barela; Karen Holmes, Bette Fairbairn, Sherrie Smith-Ferri, Director/Grace Hudson Museum and Sun House in Ukiah, California; Steve Anastasia, Loretta Farley/Park Rangers at Point Reyes National Seashore. We are especially grateful to photographer and scholar Ilka Hartmann for her photography and unendless dedication to this project.

The following is a list of the tribal affiliations of people pictured in this book: Kelly Wilmoth (Kashia Pomo), Julia Parker (Kashia Pomo/Coast Miwok), Lucy Parker (Sierra Mewük/Kashia Pomo/Coast Miwok), Sarah Brown (Pomo) with her niece Tina Fourkiller and her nephew Anthony Fourkiller, Rose Long Wolf (Pomo), Veronica Domingues (Kashia Pomo), Lanny Pinola (Kashia Pomo), Author: Edward D. Castillo (Cahuilla-Luiseño).

Library of Congress Cataloging-in-Publication Data
Castillo, Edward D.
    The Pomo/by Edward Castillo.
       p.   cm — (Indian nations)
    "A Rivilo book."
    Includes bibliographical references and index.
    Summary: Introduces the history, culture, and daily life of the Pomo Indians and examines the challenges they have faced since their first contact with Europeans.
      ISBN 0-8172-5455-2
      1. Pomo Indians Juvenile literature.   [1. Pomo Indians.   2. Indians of North America—California.]
I. Title.   II. Series: Indian nations (Austin, Tex.)
E99.P65C37   2000
979.4'0049757 — dc21   99-23200
                                         CIP

Printed and bound in the United States of America
1 2 3 4 5 6 7 8 9 0 LB 03 02 01 00

Cover photo: A Pomo girl wonders what will happen next at the California Strawberry Festival.

Contents

Creation Story

The ancestors of several bands of Indians were told of a creator spirit who appeared as a coyote. One of Coyote's first acts was to create the ocean and tide pools rich in food. Coyote then made a sweat house with the important center pole to serve as a symbolic link between this world and the spirit world. Next, Coyote collected black feathers and placed them around the sweat house facing the fire. He then changed the feathers into the First People.

Coyote declared that the First People should hold a dance and began teaching them songs. Next he ordered a feast. The festival lasted 30 days. But the people failed to honor their Creator and deeply offended him by not offering him food. Angered, Coyote lit a fire that consumed his ungrateful people.

As the fire destroyed the First People's world and began to climb mountains, Coyote commanded a rainstorm that drenched the fire and flooded the Earth. Ordering the waters to recede, Coyote began his second attempt to create the people.

Again using black feathers, Coyote created plants and animals. To keep the Earth firmly in place, Coyote raised four sacred posts at the edges of the world. He assigned male wind gods to the posts. At the same time, Coyote created a thunder god with white skin and very long hair. The god wore a buzzard-feather headdress and flopped a deerskin to make the sound of thunder.

The plants were then taught. Cottontail rabbits, gophers, and deer were told about their special abilities. Birds were

◀ *Coyote the Creator made all things.*
From feathers he made the First People.

5

shown their food and taught flying skills. The grains and acorns were taught to be food. In this manner, all of the plants and animals were shown their proper roles in the world.

Next, Coyote made the Sun and told it where and when to appear. Then Coyote declared: "The stars will be more numerous than the sands of the Earth." The Moon was made very carefully, because the Moon's duty was to help all the things on Earth to grow.

Coyote traveled from the East to the North and then to the South, around the world without stopping. Next he made a god called "Wind-man" to create wind and also medicine to help in curing ceremonies. Wind-man was given a windmill, but he made it spin too fast, causing all of the loose soil to be blown away. This created the hills that we still see today.

Coyote made more gods: for curing, for making medicines, for making daylight, and for making fire. Finally, Coyote created "Water-man" entirely of water. Water-man was to provide a place for the Sun to cool off. Suddenly, a fierce hailstorm rained down upon Coyote and Water-man, and the god "Thunder-man" reappeared from the first world that had been destroyed by fire and water. Thunder-man was told to go to the sky and

hide in the clouds and make thunder only when there was rain, hail, and clouds.

Finally the world was ready for humans. Coyote constructed several villages. He stuck four black feathers in each village and changed them into humans. The first task he assigned the Indians was to build a sweat house. Next he commanded that they hold a dance and feast—but not every day. Then he commanded them not to poison or kill one another. If this law was obeyed, then wild oats and acorns would grow in abundance, and food would be plentiful.

He next warned the humans against trespassing and stealing from neighbors. He set the proper way to ask for permission to hunt, fish, and gather. If these laws were ignored, Coyote promised again to destroy the world with both fire and rain.

Coyote then named all of the things that the people should eat, such as acorns, nuts, and fish. As the dancing and feasting began, Coyote departed, never to be seen again. From then on the humans, the animals, and the plants kept the commandments of Coyote and lived together in harmony. The Pomo world was complete.

Prehistory

Evidence of the Pomo people in northern California dates to about 1,500 years ago. Many scientists believe that many thousands of years before that, American Indians migrated during past ice ages across a land bridge from Asia, which stretched into the Americas.

It is important to understand that traditionally the Pomo, like many other American Indians, believed that they had been created in one place and had not migrated from somewhere else. To them the holy land, where the Creator walked the Earth and gave life to its many forms of life, was and is right there, in what is now called California, and not in some distant land.

Thus, the Pomo Indians had a deeply religious attachment to their territory. Even more heartfelt was their responsibility to other creatures and to make offerings to the spirits of the plants and animals that they used for food.

*This **mortar and pestle** from northern California was used to grind vegetable matter. It is thousands of years old.*

For hundreds of years before the arrival of Europeans, north of the great San Francisco Bay, the Pomo people were known by the names of their villages. The term Pomo was first recorded by government agents in 1851. It was originally applied only to a tribe on the eastern fork of the Russian River in southern Potter Valley. Pomo territory extended from the junction of the

Russian River and the coast north to the Mendocino coast near Westport. It extended into the interior to include Clear Lake, south to the plain of Santa Rosa. Summer temperatures occasionally reached 100°F (38°C), while daytime winter temperatures varied between 50 and 60°F (10 and 16°C). There was about 30 to 40 inches (76 to 102 cm) of rainfall each year. Rivers and streams were filled with salmon in the fall and steelhead in the winter. A smaller Pomo group who lived on the rugged coast had fish, clams, **abalone**, and seaweed to eat.

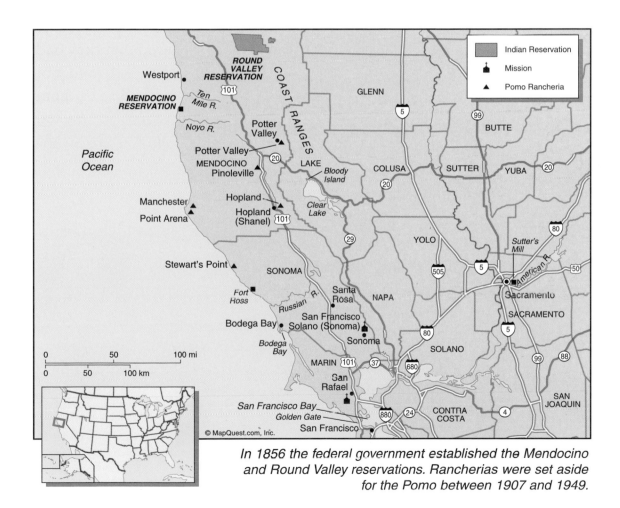

In 1856 the federal government established the Mendocino and Round Valley reservations. Rancherias were set aside for the Pomo between 1907 and 1949.

Key Historical Events

Several European sailing ships visited the Northern California Coast, beginning in 1579. The English pirate Francis Drake and two Spanish expeditions landed on the coast and encountered some Indians who may have been Pomo. The European scouting of the north coast was just the beginning of foreign invasion forces from two directions. The first came from Spanish forces to the south.

Spanish colonial policy aimed to change Indian populations into a class of landless workers serving a tiny group of Spaniards. With the help of royal Spanish troops, the missionary order of Franciscans changed the lives of many California Indians. They introduced Spanish ranching and farming methods and Roman Catholicism. Beginning in San Diego in 1769, a chain of mission

Costanoan and Coast Miwok Indians were recorded as dancing at Mission Dolores, the oldest building in San Francisco. It was established by Franciscan missionaries who attempted to convert native peoples to Christianity.

outposts and military presidios (forts) were installed along the coast. They proved to be deadly to the Indians.

The introduction of European diseases, the destruction of the natural environment, and the rounding up of nearby Indians triggered a steep population decline. These factors also created thousands of terrified refugees. Spanish sheep, horses, cattle, and hogs destroyed native plants and drove away deer, elk, and other game animals. The traditional Indian food supply dwindled rapidly, leaving tribes near colonial settlements little choice but to join mission communities. Most terrifying of all were the new diseases, against which the Indians had no immunity. From the simplest childhood sicknesses, such as measles, mumps, and chicken pox, to more devastating **plagues** of smallpox, diphtheria, pneumonia, influenza, and other various fevers, the Pomos found themselves drowning in a tidal wave of misery, suffering, and death.

In 1776 the Mission Dolores and Presidio of San Francisco were established in what is now the city of San Francisco. These and the development of nearby Mission San Rafael (1817) and San Francisco de Solano (1823) brought foreigners virtually to the doorstep of the Pomo people.

At the Presidio in 1816, Indians were forced to do hard labor for resisting Spanish rule.

The arrival of the Russian American Fur Trading Company representatives in Yerba Buena (San Francisco) in 1806 threatened Spanish control. By paying off local officials, the Russians avoided trade restrictions and were able to supply their ship with grain and vegetables for their starving outposts in Alaska. Afterward, Russians gathered a rich supply of sea otter pelts, which convinced them to establish a colony north of San Francisco Bay.

The fear of colonial rivals in the North Bay caused the Spanish in 1810 to send Lieutenant Gabriel Moraga to head troops to search for runaway mission Indians and to confirm rumors of Russians in the area. Moraga may have reached as far north as the Southern Pomo villages on the Russian River.

The next year Russians established a sea otter hunting outpost at Bodega Bay and a larger colony several miles away, called Fort Ross. The local Kashaya Pomos were friendly to the Russians, perhaps out of fear of the Spanish threat from the

Fort Ross (left) was built by Russians in 1811. It served as an outpost in their fur trade. The sea otters the Russians prized swam in waters along the rugged coast (above).

south. The Russians neither tried to convert the Pomo to their religion nor make them relocate as did the Spanish colonists.

In addition to fur trading, the Fort Ross colonists grew wheat and other farm products for their Alaskan outposts. By the 1830s, they began to kidnap Indians from the interior to help harvest their fall crops. The Indians were forced to work and were given poor rations to eat. However, temporary slavery was better than the unending slavery in the Spanish missions.

Between 1800 and 1822, Mission San Rafael succeeded in **baptizing** 3,384 North Bay Indians and recorded the deaths of 3,818. Mission San Francisco de Solano in Sonoma baptized 832 North Bay Indians and eventually buried 497.

Mexican independence finally reached California in 1822 and triggered the legal destruction of the Franciscan missions of Alta, California (north of San Diego). While technically "freeing" the Indians from Franciscan control, a corrupt class of government administrators stole mission wealth and took the land former mission Indians were promised by the padres. Surviving Indians either fled to the interior or were again enslaved by new masters who were Mexican ranchers. These ranchers called themselves "**Californios**."

After years of minor warfare, in May 1842 Salvador Vallejo, the Mexican commanding officer, led a murderous expedition into Pomo territory. It was made up of 80 Californios and an equal number of loyal Indian troops. In search of Indian slaves, Vallejo and his followers killed a number of Lake County Pomo before returning south.

We know that the Pomo endured a great smallpox plague in 1837. It started in Fort Ross and took a tremendous toll of lives. Later studies show that Russian River Pomos were dying at the rate of ten to twenty a day during the peak of the sickness.

About 1,000 Pomo and Sonoma Valley Indians died with an additional 1,000 around Clear Lake. Such a loss devastated the tiny, closely knit communities along the Russian River and became a sad memory for the Pomo people.

The treasured isolation and independence of the Pomo peoples were forever shattered. What followed tested the will and survival skills of the Pomo. Their very existence hung in the balance.

The Americans Enter

In the middle of the 19th century, relations between the United States and the poorly governed and troubled Mexican Republic became strained. The Californios faced greater Indian resistance in the form of stock raiding and attacks. Slave hunting raids by Californios were being met with fierce resistance. Many isolated ranches had to be abandoned because of Indian attacks. So desperate did Mexican California's government become that it invited many well-armed Americans to settle on the fringes of Mexican territory in order to protect recently established land grants. Americans in California grew dissatisfied under the dictatorship of Mexican rule. Soon the Americans

When enough Americans were fed up with Mexican rule in California, they rebelled and established the "Bear Flag Republic." This revolution did not help the Pomo, many of whom lived as slaves.

revolted against Mexican rule, and in June 1846 declared an independent revolutionary government called the Bear Flag Republic. This brought no help for the Pomo.

In 1847, for example, Americans Andrew Kelsey and Charles Stone arrived in Pomo territory and took over a ranch that had been owned by Mexicans. Kelsey and Stone then captured or bought hundreds of Pomos and forced them to work as slaves on the ranch. They abused, starved, sold, and even murdered Indians. (Slavery was illegal in California by 1848, but only slavery of African Americans. Indians were not protected.)

By 1850 these Pomo could no longer bear to live as slaves under Kelsey and Stone. They rose up and killed the Americans, and all the Indian people on the ranch fled into nearby hills.

Bloody Island Massacre

The Pomo hoped to come in peace and explain why they had killed the Americans, but in May 1850, an army expedition made up of 75 U.S. **dragoons** and infantry was sent to punish them. The Indians fled to an island called Badonnapati, off the extreme north shore of Clear Lake. There on May 15th, about 400 Pomo men, women, and children were attacked by the soldiers. The Army reported that between 60 and 100 Indians died in the violent attack. Indians recalled that many more, including women and children, were drowned and **bayoneted** to death, while attempting to flee or surrender at a place now called Bloody Island. Believing the Indians of Yokayo or Deep Valley to the west were also involved in the killing of Stone and Kelsey, the military force marched to the village of Cokdjal near Ukiah and slaughtered a large number of Central Pomo men, women, and children. There is no question that these were massacres. Not a single soldier lost his life in the attacks.

Sutter's Mill lies next to the south fork of the American River. The Gold Rush began there in 1848.

Gold Rush

Meanwhile, gold had been discovered on the American River on January 24, 1848. The chief of the nearby Coloma Indians warned John A. Sutter (owner of the famous mill where the Gold Rush began) that the yellow metal he so eagerly sought was "very bad medicine. It belonged to a demon who devoured all who searched for it." Soon an avalanche of misery and death descended on all California Indians.

Within a year thousands of lawless adventurers from all over the world arrived in California, with disastrous results for the state's native peoples. By the second year of the gold rush, 100,000 immigrants had arrived. Miners searched everywhere for gold. Driven by dreams of quick wealth, they had no regard for Indian land rights and were not hesitant to attack Indians on sight. Thinly spread government authorities were not able to control the miners, and all effective authority, both military and civilian, collapsed.

State Government Policy

In 1850 California's first civilian governor, John McDougall, told the new American citizens to expect "that a war of extermination will continue to be waged between the races until the Indian race becomes extinct...." Despite guarantees of the treaty ending the Mexican-American War, California Indians were denied state citizenship, voting rights, and the right to testify in court. These acts removed all legal protection for the state's native peoples and left them at the mercy of any citizen who chose to assault, kidnap, or even murder them. California had entered the Union in 1850 as a free state, but the state began passing a series of laws that had the effect of legalizing the kidnapping of Indian children and permitting a form of adult Indian slavery. Many Pomo and other tribespeople suffered under the cruel laws, until they were finally abolished four months after President Lincoln's Emancipation Proclamation of 1863 ended African American slavery across the country.

Making Treaties

Congress authorized three agents-commissioners to make treaties with the Indians of California. To accomplish this task, they were given $25,000. They arrived in California in 1851, split up, and worked in different parts of the state. They hired local interpreters and sent messages to all Indians to come and meet with them. Given the dangerous and violent conditions of Gold Rush California, many Indians regarded the request for a meeting with great suspicion and fear. The commissioners traveled with a military escort that made the Pomos especially afraid. Still, treaty commissioner Redick McKee negotiated agreements with several of the northern California tribes in the late summer of 1851.

Clear Lake supplied tule reeds used to make garments, baskets, mats, and boats. However, it became a prison for some Pomo forced to live there.

McKee and company arrived in the Pomo village of Shanel on August 21st. They met with leaders from the Yokayo and Shokowa Pomo. McKee insisted that the Central Pomo of Shokowa and the Yokayo agree to move east to Clear Lake. A treaty was negotiated the next day that promised to set aside tracts of land for the Pomo. McKee also promised the help of farmers, schoolteachers, blacksmiths, stock animals, seeds, agricultural machines, cloth, and much more in order to help the Pomo survive on the tiny treaty land on the shores of southwestern Clear Lake. With little choice, the Pomo chiefs reluctantly agreed to move within a year and surrender their ancestral home for a guaranteed reserve at Clear Lake. It was a devastating blow for the much-reduced tribe that was unable to resist the powerful newcomers. To be forced to leave their old territory with its sacred places and bones of their ancestors was like a living death for these unfortunate people.

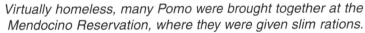

The American Period

However, in 1852 the U.S. Senate refused to ratify the treaties with the California Indians, which left the Pomo and others homeless. Everywhere the landless Indians struggled to survive as workers for the newly arrived Americans. Harsh conditions, poor health, and near-starvation led to a steady decline in the number of Pomo Indians. By 1855 nearly every part of Pomo territory was claimed by the Americans, and most of them wanted the surviving Pomo to be deported.

In 1856 the federal government established the Mendocino Reservation of 25,000 acres (10,100 ha) of land between the Noyo and Ten Mile rivers on the rugged coast. Hundreds of Pomo were rounded up and placed on that reservation. Many

Virtually homeless, many Pomo were brought together at the Mendocino Reservation, where they were given slim rations.

others were driven to Round Valley to live with other tribes. Special investigators revealed that the Indian agents were corrupt and stole funds intended to help the Pomo and other Indians. Living on the reservations or not, life was very hard during this period. Many Pomo children were kidnapped into forced labor, and working conditions were much like slavery. The Pomo were desperate and, with the exception of about a hundred at Round Valley, now entirely homeless.

The surviving Pomo set up small villages on lands they once owned and worked for local Americans when needed. Their numbers continued to drop as sicknesses, starvation, and kidnapping of their children continued.

Hard times found a village of Northern Pomo in flimsy shelters at Big River, Mendocino County, in about 1860 (left). In the early 1870s, Southeastern Pomo in the village of Elem lived in homes that were built with tule reeds (below).

The Ghost Dance

In 1870 the hopeless Pomo were drawn to a new Indian religion that predicted the end of the world and the return of all the Indians who had recently died. The new religion, called the **Ghost Dance**, promised that the Americans would disappear and Indians would again enjoy their old freedoms, health, and prosperity. New religious dances and symbols were introduced. This religious movement drew hundreds of Pomos to renew their determination to survive. The prediction that the end of the world was near was in a way true. The old world of the Pomo and other Indians was at an end. While the dead did not return, the movement helped the Pomo to adapt to their new world without entirely giving up their traditional ways.

New Homes

In 1881 four Yokayo Pomo chiefs organized their 135 followers to buy a ranch for themselves. The 120-acre (48-ha) tract of land they bought along the Russian River eventually prospered.

Kelly Wilmoth is a member of the Intertribal Pomo Dancers and Singers. She wears a headband decorated with symbols of the Ghost Dance movement.

It survives to this day as an example of what the Pomo can do for themselves. A Methodist organization purchased a ranch for the coastal Manchester Pomo Indians in 1902, and it later became a federal Indian reserve. Despite those encouraging developments, most Pomo remained homeless and suffered

Girl students at the Round Valley Indian School (above) seem to be on their best behavior. Boys at the same school (left) look ready to take off— maybe to go fishing. These children were fortunate, at least, that they did not have to go hundreds of miles away to be educated.

harsh treatment from their non-Indian neighbors. Federal Indian policy favored "civilizing" Indians by educating them in English and establishing separate schools for the Pomo and other Indian children. Some of the schools were located hundreds of miles away from their families. Pomo children were often taken from their parents and sent away for years to Indian boarding schools. This program hurt Indian families and prevented most children from learning their Pomo language and culture.

Reform

In about 1900 a new generation of Pomo leadership began working with reform organizations, using the courts and even newspapers to seek more humane treatment. Because they were landless and constantly subjected to evictions from their villages, a permanent land base was essential for Pomo survival. The United States government finally responded by seeking to help landless California Indians in 1906. Between 1907 and 1949, 16 **rancherias** (or home sites of several hundred acres or less) were established for them. Almost none of these lands possessed any resources. Only a handful of residents could earn a living by either ranching or farming on them.

To help the Pomo adjust to 20th-century life, local segregated Indian schools were established in several places near their rancherias. After World War I, Pomo leaders, with the help of some civil rights groups, sued local school boards to allow Indian children to attend public schools. They won, though the schools were segregated—for Indians only. Non-reservation Pomos sued Mendocino County for the right to vote and eventually won their case.

Way of Life

Before Europeans came, the Pomo collected wild foods and hunted, trapped, and fished. Their major staple was acorns, which grew ripe in the fall and were harvested in vast quantities. Seven different types of acorns were collected. Various seeds, berries, and 15 different grass seeds, roots, and greens were harvested. Many of these were eaten immediately, while others were stored for trade or for eating later. Women skillfully constructed beautiful baskets to use for collecting foods. A stone mortar and pestle for grinding seeds and nuts was in every home.

Most harvesting of seeds, berries, and fruits was done by women, and this made perfect sense to the Pomo. With women's highly prized power to bring new life into the world by giving birth, it seemed natural that they would gather food that did not involve killing.

Men's duties, however, required them to kill animals. Hunting tools included the bow and

At the Native American Spring Gathering in Santa Rosa, California, Julia Parker (above) demonstrates how to grind acorns using a mortar and pestle of natural stone. This woman (left) gathers seeds to dry and crush into a meal called pinole.

24

arrow for large game animals, dip nets and fishing lines for fish, and various traps and snares for small animals. Birds were hunted for food and sometimes for their feathers. However, the killing of hawks, loons, crows, seagulls, and owls was forbidden. Rabbits and squirrels were hunted, and big game animals, such as elk, antelope, deer, and sea lions, were much prized. A successful hunt required that strict religious rules be followed. Hunting gear was blessed, prayers and thanks were offered, and the hunted animals were asked for forgiveness.

Group deer hunts featured a hunter wearing a **decoy head**. He was assisted by others who drove the deer near the hunter and helped him carry out the kill. Slain deer were usually cut up on the spot and divided among participants. A recently married hunter, however, was expected to take the entire animal to his mother-in-law, where it was butchered at her home.

Steelhead, salmon, and trout were caught in great numbers from the Russian, Eel, Petaluma, and Sonoma rivers and from neighboring creeks. Sometimes at night a dam was constructed across a river, and a gap was left at the deepest end where a fisherman with a dip net scooped up his catch. Other times, fishermen waded into the water and took salmon with harpoons. As in hunting, a ritual thanks was given to the fish, and fishing gear was ritually cleansed.

Men's duties included hunting for small and big game. While fishing for salmon, they often used harpoons.

Once the acorns are ground, Julia Parker will soak the meal in water to remove tannic acid from the nuts.

Food

Acorns were stored in large baskets in the home. The acorns were shelled, ground into a meal, and water was poured over the meal to rinse out **tannic acid**. The resulting porridge was baked on heated stones to make nutritious bread or was boiled into a soup. The porridge was often sweetened with berries or mixed with other foods for additional flavoring and nutrition.

Birds' eggs were collected to eat while still fresh, and hunted birds were roasted or baked. Fish not eaten right away were split and laid out to dry with the aid of a fire. Then they were stored in baskets.

Trade Feasts

When food was abundant, villagers might host a trade feast. The chief of the host village would send a good runner with an invitation to other villages.

Upon arrival, the guest chief offered a sack of clamshell money saying, "Help yourself to a few beads." He then made a short speech to express the importance of friendship and good relations between their villages. The host village chief welcomed the guests, and several days of celebration, including sweat ceremonies, dances, and gambling, began.

The Pomo seldom traded with strangers. Strict rules of hospitality, however, permitted strangers to enter a home. The stranger could choose whatever he or she wanted and offer any amount of clamshell money. The host had to accept the offer, even if it was unfair. But if the deal was grossly unfair, the seller had the right to confront the buyer the next day.

When one village was host to another, a welcome line was set up. In about 1902 dancers await visitors before a dance house in Clear Lake.

Modern ceremonial dancers from Ukiah, California, called YOKAYO. Traditional Pomo dancers wore detailed necklaces, headdresses, feathers, skins, and painted designs on their bodies.

Clothing and Adornment

Because of California's mild climate, the Pomo wore little clothing. In warm springs and hot summers, men often went without any clothes, but **breechclouts** were worn when hunting and during ceremonial activities. Poorer men wore capes of shredded willow bark during cold and rainy weather, while higher status males wore capes made from small animal skins stitched together. Women always wore skirts that wrapped at the waist and extended to the ankles. For women of lesser status, the skirts were made of shredded willow bark, while their wealthier neighbors wore deerskin skirts. In very cold weather, both sexes might don rabbit-skin blankets. These were worn like robes and fastened by wooden pins. Other cold weather blankets were made from the skins of sea otters, bears, mountain lions, and wildcats. On ceremonial occasions, the wealthy dressed in finely manufactured feather capes and sashes. Clamshell beads, **magnesite** cylinders, and abalone pendants were worn as belts, necklaces, and wristbands. Ceremonial dancers wore breechclouts and elaborate abalone **chokers** and **flicker** feather headdresses.

Structures

Multifamily houses were built in circular, egg-shaped, or L-shaped patterns. Some houses could hold as many as 12 to 30 people. Willow poles about 2 inches (5 cm) in diameter were driven into the ground, and a **lattice** framework of smaller poles was tied to them using ropes made from twisted fibers. **Thatching** the house made it waterproof. A low door and a smoke hole in the ceiling provided a doorway and proper ventilation. The house was surrounded by a brush fence where acorns were hung to dry.

Each village had at least one small building in which sweat baths were held. A circular hole was dug, around which was built a pole-frame structure. This was covered with brush and then compacted with earth.

In a Pomo home, a man repairs a net while women prepare to boil ground corn in a basket.

The round house was the largest structure found in a village. Like the sweat house, it was constructed over a shallow pit in the earth, but because of its size, it was constructed of heavy timber. The main structure was circular in shape and averaged about 70 feet (21 m) across. Eight upright timbers located in a circle around the interior dance area acted as roof supports. A sacred pole stood in the center. A small door in the back, opposite the main entrance, allowed dancers to enter and exit. Earth was compacted around the walls and on the roof, making the building look like a large earth mound. Spectators sat on soft, freshly cut plant material. These structures served as village assembly halls and dramatic settings for colorful ceremonies.

Basketry

Pomo baskets are recognized today as among the finest ever produced. Museums around the world display many examples of the artfully woven and often highly decorated baskets. Throughout the Americas women were principally responsible for producing baskets. However, Pomo males did construct a type that they used for trapping birds and fish. Men also made baskets for sale in order to raise money when necessary.

Superior Pomo basketry included deep, bowl-shaped vessels for storage (right). Boat-shaped baskets (below) were often given as prized gifts.

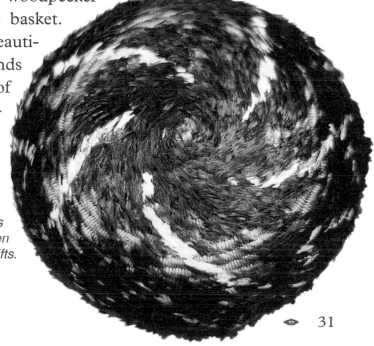

The great majority of baskets were used for storing seeds and other dried foods. The driving force for their manufacture was acorn gathering and the processing demands of the collecting done by Pomo peoples. For instance, special baskets were made for straining foods and separating seeds from their husks.

Like other California Indians, the Pomo used their baskets for cooking. The baskets were so tightly woven that they could hold water. Finely ground acorn meal mixed with water was poured into them. Small, round stones were heated in a fire, carefully brushed to remove ashes, and lifted into the basket with special sticks (used like chopsticks). The contents of the basket were quickly stirred to prevent the hot stones from scorching the interior. In a few minutes, the contents boiled. Next, the stones were removed, and the nourishing mush was served with mussel-shell spoons.

The most spectacular Pomo basketry were special gift baskets decorated with clamshell beads and feathers. Feathers of mallard ducks, meadowlarks, blackbirds, blue jays, and robins, as well as quail and woodpecker crests, were woven into the basket. Some of these delicate and beautiful works of art featured bands of feathers around the lip of the baskets. Especially valuable baskets were completely covered with feathers. Only

Among the finest of all baskets were those decorated with beads and feathers, which were often wedding gifts.

31

certain selected feathers of a bird could be used. For a completely covered basket of about 10 inches (25 cm) in diameter, the special feathers of hundreds of birds had to be used.

A very special kind of Pomo basketry staggers the imagination—miniatures ranging in size from 2 inches (5 cm) across to the size of the head of a pin. To see the smallest ones clearly, you need a magnifying glass. The techniques that are used to produce them remain a closely guarded secret. Fortunately Pomo basketmaking has survived.

A basket can be designed to be large and beautiful, even while it is still being made (left). Some miniature gift or medicine baskets were made so incredibly tiny that an apple dwarfs them (below).

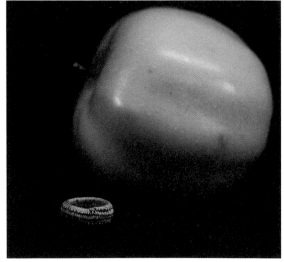

Spiritual Life

The Pomo believed that the plants, animals, and places of their territory had living spirits that must be honored. Sickness and misfortune could be caused by violating various **taboos** or by ghosts, or by witches' **"poisoning"**—placing a curse or supernatural spell. To cure such problems, it was necessary to have the help of a **shaman**, or Indian doctor, skilled in the healing arts. Curing specialists provided herbal medicines. Singing doctors used magical artifacts of stone and bone as well as singing to cure sickness. In extreme cases, important religious leaders called kuksu provided supernatural curing.

Health and prosperity could be achieved by prayer, charms, and various ceremonies. Some Pomo peoples had a variety of medicines, the secrets of which had been handed down in families. Sometimes the secrets were in the form of songs, and other times they were in the form of special ceremonial clothing. **Angelica root** and other herbs were rubbed on the skin of hunters for good luck and protection. Pepperwood leaves were also rubbed on hunting equipment for good luck.

In 1898 Grace C. Hudson painted her version of Jack (Napoleon), a spiritual leader of the Pomo community at Pinoleville. He calls the Creator "to come and guide the spirit of the dead to the end of the earth."

The Coyote's Coming, 1898 oil on canvas 24 x 18, Grace Hudson Museum, gift of the Ivan B. and Elvira Hart Trust

Ceremonies

Ceremonies were organized by officials, usually the village chiefs. But other people, such as an especially successful hunter or a particularly popular female, might host a ceremony. Important to each ceremony were supporting officials such as fire tenders, head singers, drummers, chorus singers, and the master of ceremonies.

When these officials decided to host a ceremony or **ritual**, a **crier** walked through the village informing the people of their chiefs' decision. Neighboring villages were invited by runners who carried invitations consisting of wormwood or willow sticks tied with short strings. The number of sticks indicated the number of days until the event would occur. The runner would then return with the confirmation of the guests' acceptances. Visiting tribes usually arrived a day before and camped outside of the host village. On the morning of the ceremony, the visitors marched into the village. Visiting chiefs led and carried **shell bead money**. The host's village chief emerged from the ceremonial round house and personally greeted his guests. The guest chief then made a short speech and presented the host chief with the shell bead money.

The head singer was vital to the success of all ceremonies, because his responsibility was to organize the proper sequences of dances and songs. He began the songs and set the tempo.

Shells were processed into money or jewelry by drilling clam fragments and shaping them into beads.

At the California Strawberry Festival, berries are traditionally fed to guests as they leave. Private ceremonies are held in a special structure (left) at Stewart's Point Rancheria.

Ceremonies always took place in the Ceremonial house and usually lasted four nights. Events began after sunset. The head singer gave a blessing to open the proceedings. Dancing by men and women in ceremonial dress followed. Throughout the ceremony, a feast was enjoyed by participants and the audience. Finally, a series of speeches were made, and a purification ritual or sweat bath brought things to an end.

Other public rituals were performed specifically to offer thanks for a good harvest of acorns, manzanita (evergreen shrubs), wild strawberries, and other foods.

Tribal Society

Almost every Indian society in California had social classes. Status was based on one's family, background, wealth, and individual achievement. Social status might also be helped by membership in religious societies. Chiefs were the highest ranked. Ritual leaders also enjoyed high status. Just below the ritual leaders were shamans. Also below the ritual leaders were less powerful Indian doctors and people who might now and then serve as minor ritual leaders. Special status was also given to others, including shell bead makers, hunters, and special craftspeople, such as bow and basket makers.

Considerable power rested in families. They were free to move to neighboring villages and maintain territorial rights in their old homes. The government of Pomo peoples was organized around the family. Each village was ruled by extended

At the Strawberry Festival in Kule Loklo, California, younger women dance facing older women and honor them in a ceremony.

family chiefs functioning as a council. Villages were independent political units. Nevertheless, several communities often acted as a **confederation** for trade or war. Major chiefs were advisers, met visitors, presided over meetings with minor chiefs, arranged ceremonial events, and made peace at the end of an armed conflict. Minor chicfs looked after the interest of their families and distributed foods collected by communal groups. Women who were closely related to a former chief sometimes became chiefs themselves.

War

War among the Pomo Indians seldom led to deaths. The main cause of war was a belief that members of another tribe had poisoned (cursed) someone. Other causes included disputes over tribal boundaries and fishing rights, **poaching** game, or the kidnapping of women and children.

Pomo territories, such as this oak woodland on the east side of Sonoma Mountain, were rich with food and other valuable resources that often had to be defended from outsiders.

War parties might number as many as three hundred men on each side. Warriors painted the areas around their mouths and cheeks with charcoal to give them the terrifying look of skeletons, and sometimes they wore buzzard-feather head-dresses. Weapons included bows and arrows, thrusting spears, and slings (slingshots).

During the journey toward the battlefield, the war chief would stop the party, smoke his pipe, and in a prayer offer shell beads to the Sun. He would ask the spirits for a successful campaign. The entire group would then shout the war cry "Ui-he" (WE-HEE) four times, and the journey resumed.

Usually, battles were prearranged affairs requiring each side to form a single line of warriors facing the opposing party, with the war chiefs in the center. Each side would charge, then retreat, all the while taunting opponents and boasting of their own power. When an enemy was wounded, the opposing side would send up a chorus of howls of triumph. Women and children stayed well behind the action, supplying rocks for their warriors' slings.

If one side broke and began to retreat to its own territory, the winners would shout, "Stay home and be good!" In rare cases the winning side might chase their enemies back to their village and burn it. Most wars were resolved by peace treaties. It was the responsibility of the opposing chiefs to make peace.

Contemporary Life

Hundreds of Pomo men enlisted in the armed services during World War II. Many Pomo women left their reservations and worked in war industries as far away as San Francisco and Los Angeles.

After the war, Pomos grew impatient with the **Bureau of Indian Affairs (B.I.A.)**, which controlled their tribal funds and decisions. Veterans had witnessed the generous assistance the United States had provided in rebuilding the countries of former enemies. Pomos reasoned that if the United States could afford to spend billions of dollars rebuilding Germany and Japan, it ought to help American Indian communities. Even so, discrimination against Indians, the seasonal nature of the farm work, general poor health, and lack of medical care continued to make life very difficult for most Indians until about 1970.

Tribal Government

With the establishment of reservations, each community set up a governing council. Most followed the U. S. Constitution, allowing all men and women voting rights to elect tribal councils and chiefs. But the most important decisions for their reservations were still made by the B.I.A. As in the past, this federal agency really controlled Pomo

Sarah Brown takes care of her niece and nephew, Tina and Anthony Fourkiller, at the Intertribal Friendship House in Oakland, California.

governments by funding favored leaders and their plans but opposing an Indian decision when it did not please the B.I.A. Despite this disadvantage, Pomo leaders struggled to improve housing, health, and roads and to provide clean drinking water for their members.

Education

Educational achievement was poor until recent years. Many Pomo parents bitterly remembered the cruel boarding schools and segregated classrooms in public schools. They saw little hope in their children's ability to stand up to the teachers, and they felt that textbooks contained many untrue and hurtful things about Indians or ignored them altogether. In recent years things have changed for the better. School books are more accurate, and many teachers now value Indian students and their culture.

Today many Pomo have completed college and hold responsible positions in tribal governments as well as state and national Indian leadership roles. Joseph Meyers is a Pinoleville Pomo

Rose Long Wolf and her children, April, Lorenda, and Theodora, take time out at the Strawberry Festival to relax.

attorney who heads a corporation that trains tribal judges. Larry Meyers is the Executive Secretary of the California Native American Heritage Commission. This group protects Indian religious freedoms and Indian burial grounds.

Veronica Domingues, one of the author's students, advances in Sonoma State's Native Studies program.

The Future

Pomo traditions have survived and now have wide support by Pomo youth. Several dance groups continue to perform sacred ceremonies and sometimes dance just for fun. Many Pomo youth enjoy traditional dancing and singing and making beautiful ceremonial outfits. Pomo basketmakers continue to excel in their traditional art and to train young basketmakers.

The future outlook for the Pomo people is perhaps the best it has been in more than a century. Dedicated tribal leaders have taken control of their future. They have secured improved housing, education, and health services for their tribal members. Traditional Pomo culture is proudly practiced. Five Pomo rancherias have set up gaming casinos. Because of these casinos, many Pomo for the first time have a steady income for their communities and also for their members.

Lanny Pinola is a respected spiritual elder and park ranger at Point Reyes National Park (left). Concentrating intensely, a Pomo boy gives new energy to an old dance (right). He embodies a Pomo ideal: "Honoring our children by honoring our traditions."

Pomo Recipe

Modern Pomo Acorn Soup

Collect acorns in the fall when they ripen. Store them in a dry place for several weeks or even months. Remove the shells from the acorns, and put them in a blender. Blend the dry acorns into a smooth, powdery meal. Put the meal in some cheesecloth. Place it in a colander. Soak for 30 minutes, rinsing every now and

Acorns from a coast live oak

then with lukewarm water. From time to time, taste the wet meal until it no longer tastes bitter. Place the meal in a saucepan, and add water and salt to taste. Heat slowly, until the meal thickens. Serve in a cup. Add strawberries or blueberries for a sweeter taste.

Acorn meal shown after the soaking and rinsing process

Pomo Chronology

A.D. 500	Oldest evidence of the Pomo tribe thus far.
1579	English pirate Francis Drake camps on the beach near Southern Pomo villages and hosts Indian visitors.
1595	Spanish explorer Rodriguez Cermenho explores Pomo coasts near Cape Mendocino.
1810	Spanish military officer Gabriel Moraga enters Pomo territory near Russian River looking for Indian runaways from the missions.
1811	Russian American Fur Company establishes colony at Fort Ross on Kashaya Pomo Coast.
1817	Mission San Rafael is established, and the first Pomo Indians are baptized.
	Russians and Pomo sign a Treaty of Peace and Friendship.
1834	Pomo Chief Succara battles Mexican and Indian troops seeking Pomo slaves.
1837	Smallpox kills thousands of Pomo and others in nearby tribes.
1842	Salvador Vallejo invades Pomo lands seeking slaves.
1848	Several hundred Pomo men are kidnapped and taken to the gold mining district. Only a dozen survive.
1850	Lake County Pomo kill two Americans who abused them and kidnapped their women.
	The U.S. Army massacres several hundred Pomo men, women, and children at Clear Lake and Deep Valley to punish the Pomo for killing two Americans.
	State government legalizes Indian slavery. Hundreds of Pomo are kidnapped and enslaved by Americans.
1851	Pomo leaders sign a treaty with the United States government. Congress refuses to agree, and treaties are not enacted. All Indians are now landless.

1856	Mendocino and Round Valley reservations are established for Pomo and other Indians.
1863	Slavery is outlawed by the U.S. Government. Several years pass before this law is enforced for Indians in California.
1870	A powerful Indian religious revival known as the Ghost Dance spreads among the Pomo.
1881	Yokayo Pomo of Deep Valley pool their money and buy a farm. It is successful and exists to this day.
1907	The Bureau of Indian Affairs purchases 16 separate areas of land between 1907 and 1949 for landless Pomo Indians.
1918	Non-Reservation Pomos sue school officials to allow Indian children to attend public schools.
1924	All Pomo Indians and other Indians born in the United States are made U.S. citizens.
1926	First all-Indian civil rights organization in California, called the California Indian Brotherhood, is established by Pomo leader Stephen Knight.
1928	Pomo Indians sue the federal government for the theft of their lands. A very unfair settlement is made in 1944.
1961	The Bureau of Indian Affairs tricks 11 Pomo rancherias into agreeing to end their federal protection status called Federal Trust. The majority of the communities involved lost all of their lands to tax debts.
1970	Pomo Indians occupy and eventually receive the right to a government spy facility in Forestville, California. They establish an Indian Education Center called Ya-Ka-Ama (Our Land).
1988	The first Pomo Indian gaming facility is established at Coyote Valley Rancheria.
1994	Elsie Allen High School is dedicated in Santa Rosa, California, to the world-famous Pomo basketmaker. This is the only public school named after a California Indian.

Glossary

Abalone A type of rock-clinging mollusk. It has a flattened shell lined with mother-of-pearl.

Angelica root A root found in Pomo territory that is used by Indian doctors and medicine men to cure many forms of sickness.

Attorney A lawyer.

Baptizing A ritual performed using water. It admits one to the Christian community.

Bayoneted To be stuck with a bayonet, or knife attached to a rifle.

Breechclout A short piece of clothing worn like trunks by men.

Bureau of Indian Affairs (B.I.A.) The department of the United States Federal Government that is supposed to support, defend, and help Indian people in the United States.

Californios Mexican colonists who were born in California.

Chokers Necklaces of shells and shaped stones that are used in ceremonial dress.

Confederation An association or union made to further the common interests of its members.

Crier One who makes public proclamations as instructed by a chief or leader.

Decoy heads Stuffed, large animal heads tied to the head of a hunter.

Dragoons Army troops mounted on horseback.

Flicker A North American woodpecker. The Pomo used flicker feathers to make ceremonial headdresses.

Ghost Dance A special dance performed to ask the spirits of the dead not to be angry with the living for disrespectful behavior.

Lattice A framework or structure of crossed wood or metal strips.

45

Magnesite A white salt made of crystal that occurs naturally.

Mortar and pestle A shallow-shaped rock bowl and a hand-shaped grinding rock. Together they were used to grind acorns into meal.

Plagues New and deadly diseases that spread rapidly.

Poaching Killing game animals in another village's territory. It is a crime and cause for war.

Poisoning A form of Indian witchcraft. It is similar to casting a spell on a person.

Rancherias Indian lands that are similar to reservations but smaller.

Ritual Repeated, often formal, acts that are customary.

Shaman A person who is a religious leader and cures sickness among the tribespeople.

Shell bead money A form of both jewelry and money. It is the difficult and time-consuming production of shattered clam shells into beads shaped like buttons with a single hole.

Taboos Acts that are prohibited according to social custom.

Tannic acid The natural acid found in acorns that must be rinsed out so that the acorns will not taste bitter.

Thatching Plant material used as a sheltering cover, such as a roof.

The author, Edward D. Castillo (left), with his son, Andrew K. Castillo, who in addition to his dad's tribe, is also a member of the Pomo tribe of Round Valley, California.

Further Reading

Dominic, Gloria. *Coyote and the Grasshoppers: A Pomo Legend* (Native American Lore and Legends series). Rourke, 1997.

Landau, Elaine. *The Pomo*. Danbury, CT: Franklin Watts, 1997.

Lund, Bill. *The Pomo Indians* (Native Peoples series). Bridgestone, 1997.

Viola, Herman J. *North American Indians: An Introduction to the Lives of America's Native Peoples, from the Inuit of the Arctic to the Zuni of the Southwest*. New York: Crown, 1996.

Sources

Able-Vidor, D. Bovarney, and S. Billy. *Remember Your Relations. The Elsie Allen Baskets, Family and Friends*. Ukiah, CA: Grace Hudson Museum, 1996.

Allen, Elsie. *Pomo Basketmaking, A Supreme Art of the Weaver*. Happy Camp, CA: Naturegraph Publishers, 1972.

Barrett, Samuel. *Pomo Myths*. Bulletin of the Public Museum of the City of Milwaukee 15. Milwaukee, WI: 1933.

Brown, Vinson, and Douglas Andrews. *The Pomo Indians of California and Their Neighbors*. Heraldsburg, CA: Naturegraph Publishers, 1969.

Goodrich, Jennie, Claudia Lawson, and Vanna Parrish Lawson. *Kashaya Pomo Plants*. Berkeley CA: Heyday Books, 1998.

Heizer, Robert F. *Handbook of the Indians of North America*, Vol. 8 California. Washington, D.C.: Smithsonian Institution Press, pp. 274–323, 1978.

Oswalt, Robert L. *Kashaya Texts. University of California Publications in Linguistics*. Berkeley, CA: University of California Press.

Sarris, Greg. *Mabel McKay: Weaving the Dream*. Berkeley, CA: University of California Press, 1995.

Index

Numbers in italics indicate illustration or map.